Single But NOT Satisfied

For Mature Singles with a Desire for Marriage

Funmi Quadri-Jimoh

WestBow Press
A DIVISION OF THOMAS NELSON
& ZONDERVAN

Copyright © 2018 Funmi Quadri-Jimoh.

All rights reserved. No part of this book may be used or reproduced by any means, graphic, electronic, or mechanical, including photocopying, recording, taping or by any information storage retrieval system without the written permission of the author except in the case of brief quotations embodied in critical articles and reviews.

WestBow Press books may be ordered through booksellers or by contacting:

WestBow Press
A Division of Thomas Nelson & Zondervan
1663 Liberty Drive
Bloomington, IN 47403
www.westbowpress.com
1 (866) 928-1240

Because of the dynamic nature of the Internet, any web addresses or links contained in this book may have changed since publication and may no longer be valid. The views expressed in this work are solely those of the author and do not necessarily reflect the views of the publisher, and the publisher hereby disclaims any responsibility for them.

Any people depicted in stock imagery provided by Getty Images are models, and such images are being used for illustrative purposes only.
Certain stock imagery © Getty Images.

ISBN: 978-1-9736-3527-7 (sc)
ISBN: 978-1-9736-3528-4 (e)

Print information available on the last page.

WestBow Press rev. date: 09/25/2018

THE HOLY BIBLE, NEW INTERNATIONAL VERSION®, NIV® Copyright © 1973, 1978, 1984, 2011 by Biblica, Inc.® Used by permission. All rights reserved worldwide.

The Living Bible copyright © 1971 by Tyndale House Foundation. Used by permission of Tyndale House Publishers Inc., Carol Stream, Illinois 60188. All rights reserved. The Living Bible, TLB, and the The Living Bible logo are registered trademarks of Tyndale House Publishers.

Scripture taken from the Common English Bible®, CEB® Copyright © 2010, 2011 by Common English Bible.™ Used by permission. All rights reserved. No part of these materials may be reproduced or transmitted in any form or by any means, electronic or mechanical, including photocopying and recording, or by any information storage or retrieval system, except as may be expressly permitted by the 1976 Copyright Act, the 1998 Digital Millennium Copyright Act, or in writing from the publisher.

Scripture taken from the Amplified Bible. Copyright © 2015 by The Lockman Foundation, La Habra, CA 90631. All rights reserved. For Permission To Quote information visit http://www.lockman.org

The Jubilee Bible (from the Scriptures of the Reformation) edited by Russell M. Stendal. Copyright © 2000, 2001, 2010

Scripture quotations marked HCSB are taken from the Holman Christian Standard Bible®, Copyright © 1999, 2000, 2002, 2003, 2009 by Holman Bible Publishers. Used by permission. Holman Christian Standard Bible®, Holman CSB®, and HCSB® are federally registered trademarks of Holman Bible Publishers.

Scripture taken from the New King James Version®. Copyright © 1982 by Thomas Nelson. Used by permission. All rights reserved.

Scripture quotations marked NLT are taken from the Holy Bible, New Living Translation, copyright © 1996, 2004, 2015 by Tyndale House Foundation. Used by permission of Tyndale House Publishers, Inc., Carol Stream, Illinois 60188. All rights reserved.

Scripture is taken from GOD'S WORD®, © 1995 God's Word to the Nations. Used by permission of Baker Publishing Group.

Scripture taken from the Modern English Version. Copyright © 2014 by Military Bible Association. Used by permission. All rights reserved.

The ESV® Bible (The Holy Bible, English Standard Version®). ESV® Text Edition: 2016. Copyright © 2001 by Crossway, a publishing ministry of Good News Publishers. The ESV® text has been reproduced in cooperation with and by permission of Good News Publishers. Unauthorized reproduction of this publication is prohibited. All rights reserved.

The Christian Standard Bible. Copyright © 2017 by Holman Bible Publishers. Used by permission. Christian Standard Bible®, and CSB® are federally registered trademarks of Holman Bible Publishers, all rights reserved.

Contemporary English Version® Copyright © 1995 American Bible Society. All rights reserved.

Scripture taken from The Message. Copyright © 1993, 1994, 1995, 1996, 2000, 2001, 2002. Used by permission of NavPress Publishing Group.

Scripture quotations taken from the Amplified® Bible (AMPC), Copyright © 1954, 1958, 1962, 1964, 1965, 1987 by The Lockman Foundation. Used by permission. www.Lockman.org

DEDICATION

Lord you said that if I commit my works to you, you would establish them and make my plans succeed. Proverbs 16:2

ACKNOWLEDGEMENTS

I acknowledge the Holy Spirit and his help in writing this book, a million thanks for everything. I appreciate my exceptional husband and prayer partner Olayiwola, you are a major blessing, there are bigger victories ahead of us. My excellent and 'well favoured' son Emmanuel, you are an evidence of God's benevolence and providence.

My brother and his wife, Pastors Tunde and Bussy Okeowo, for decades of love and support. My sister and her husband, Oludola and Idowu Badejo, for your tenacity and tireless effort in prayer, I appreciate you dearly. My uncle, Olusola Adesanya, you are a hero. Minister Tunde Disu, my brother from another mother, for your consistent mentoring and encouragement. You have set me on this book writing path.

Pastors Jerome and Ruth Anekwe, my outstanding Pastors, your commitment to the word is commendable, thank you for standing with me all these years. I am a partaker of your grace and a testimony of your assignment.

My family at Destiny Christian Centre London, you are so special and finally my mother, Olubunmi Okeowo, who relocated to heaven in December 2016, I miss you dearly, thank you for all your labour in prayer, I am eternally grateful.

CONTENTS

Chapter 1: Introduction 1
Chapter 2: God is Pro Marriage 5
Chapter 3: Satan's lies 12
Chapter 4: The favour factor 20
Chapter 5: Your spiritual network matters 26
Chapter 6: Get rid of blockers 30
Chapter 7: Those you should not date or marry 35
Chapter 8: Maximise your life 40
Chapter 9: Pray, Pray and Pray 45
Chapter 10: Testimonies 54
    Testimony 1: Married for the first time at 52 54
    Testimony 2: Divorced but remembered 59
    Testimony 3: Single but NOT satisfied 66

PROLOGUE

Dancing with my husband at the reception of our wedding at the Sheraton hotel, today is the 30th day of October of the year of the Lord. I am getting married at long last for the very first time at the age of 43 to a good man who is also getting married for the first time at the age of 47. It is all playing out before my eyes, God fulfilling his own end of our bargain… now I must fulfil my own part …to document his faithfulness and empower others. One of the reasons God gave me a spouse is to help his children get their own spouses. 2 Corinthians 1:4.

Ladies and gentlemen, your time is now…

Every time God has given me the opportunity to address mature singles, my opening line has been the same everywhere: Singleness (for most Christians) is only a blessing until you reach a certain age. This 'certain age' differs from culture to culture. After that 'certain age' singleness becomes a reproach and a major prayer point, and unless you have the Paul 'eunuch-like' calling in life, there is a desire to marry and to enjoy the blessing of companionship and marriage.

For most Christians today, people often accept that is still okay to marry in the late 20s to early 30s. After this age the phrases 'old maid' and 'confirmed bachelor' are used to describe those who fall into the single category.

I noticed that most people that pontificate singleness as a blessing are often married. If God wanted us to be single, surely he would not put the desire for a relationship in our hearts and he would have left Adam to sort himself out rather than create a helper suitable for him.

My understanding is that a lack by any name is still a lack regardless of what shape or form it comes in; lack of health, lack of a job, lack of money, lack of vision, lack of children, lack of husband, lack of a wife… all constitute a lack. And we as Christians have been taught to 'attack our lack'.

The lack of a spouse however does not get the same reaction as the other lacks in the church community. If someone came into our church meeting and said he had a tumour (lack of health) and requested prayer, the whole church will take a very aggressive stance against this situation and pray with all their might. They would immediately recognise this as an affliction from the enemy and will agree with the person afflicted to drive out this devil; however if someone requested a prayer to be married, it is not treated with the same degree of urgency. It is treated with a more casual attitude, it is treated as a social issue. Often those in this type of situation are encouraged to 'socialise' and be 'more active' in their churches, and to serve God with more tenacity. It is often seen as a natural 'issue' and often addressed as one.

Many churches organise singles social events to encourage 'the singles to mingle' but very few of these events produce the desired results. Often there are more ladies than men attending these events, month over month and year on year and there is no change to their circumstances.

Have you ever wondered why a Christian with no disability, no natural defect, good looking, good job, bright future and even a diligent worker in the church is single? Have you ever wondered why there are so many single Christian ladies? Singleness after a certain age is not a natural issue and should not be seen or addressed as one, in most cases there is a spiritual cause that needs to be shifted (as was my own case) for the marriage to happen.

I am a firm believer that God want us to have all that pertains to life and Godliness and if that includes being married then we have a right to it. As you read this book, please know that God has a plan for your life and it is a good plan.

CHAPTER 1

INTRODUCTION

Sitting in my bedroom in Toronto Canada on the faithful day when I turned thirty-five years old; thirty-five years since I was born on this planet and I have been a Christian for more than half of it.

I was born again at the very early age of fifteen and was filled with the Holy Spirit when I was in boarding school the year after. I became a fervent Christian almost immediately with what many will term a contagious faith. I loved the Lord intensely and was committed to propagating the gospel of Jesus.

Now… Fast forward 20 years after, I still loved God with my whole heart and served diligently within the local church. I was an active cell leader, loved outreaches and a firm believer of the word… but why was I still single? It was with this thought that I woke up on my 35th birthday, I cried like a baby I felt like God had forgotten me. Where did all the time go?

What was I doing wrong? Why was I still single? Why the delay? What could I have done better? I was born into a middle class African family where education was a must. It was mandatory to be educated to a degree level and any other way was not an option.

I was qualified account with a master's degree in finance. I was not a beauty queen, but I was not Godzilla either. I dressed smartly, had a good job and drove a good car, spoke well… so why was I still single?

A dear friend of mine shared my condo with me at that time and she also looked up to me as a Christian mentor. She wept alongside with me that day, knowing how much I longed to be married. The future looked very bleak as everywhere I turned I saw married men; Canada is quite a family-oriented country so been single was the exception rather than the rule. Single men were as scarce as the Canadian summer.

I had moved to Canada 7 years before, in my quest to live somewhere else. Even though it was initially challenging, I eventually settled down. My pastors were excellent and supportive; they are still close friends till today. I also had close praying friends (funny enough, all are pastors and church leaders today). On the surface I had the entire spiritual support and network that anyone needed to have a good quality of life, so why was I still single?

I was not an introvert; I loved life and travelled extensively, thanks to my consulting job. I was never lonely and whenever I was alone it was by choice. I had friends and was friendly; thankfully God had blessed me with a good smile. But this did not quench the desire for a marital relationship. I was single and NOT satisfied. I knew God had a plan and I was not going to exit this planet without it. The million $ question is, why was I still single?

There were more women in the church I attended as in most churches, but it seems like the most diligent/faithful ones were the single ones. Something seems to be wrong somewhere and if you are like me you will start to ask God questions, what am I not doing right? What have I not done? When will it be my turn?

After I turned thirty-six I made up my mind to break the routine of living a triangular life i.e. work, home, and church. My life was full of church work and infrequent social events. I made up my mind to start socialising, thinking that will help to get a man (this really helps at times, but it is not the answer).

Canada's main social event in the winter was skating, I decided to learn to skate and be more social but very quickly realised these types of people were not the type I wanted to spend the rest of my life with, they had no regard for God and the things of the spirit, we were not operating on the same spiritual frequency.

At this junction, most of my friends were married and had children so most of the conversation revolved around their home, kids, after-school clubs, camps and it was surely not 'raining men' in Toronto.

I was not just a regular Christian; I was a 'word of faith' pedigree. I loved the word of God, believed and embraced the work of the Holy Spirit and therefore could not quite understand how a loving God who loved to save, heal and deliver was not able to provide a husband. A generous father who gave his only son, surely a good husband was not too hard for him.

Thankfully I was in a word-based church that moved in gifting of the Holy Spirit and the gifts of healing. I was privileged to be a part of the healing school and was a key participant in the organisation and administration of one of the healing meetings, so I had the advantage of seeing the power of God move on people's bodies especially when they had the faith to be healed. So, if God could restore deaf ears, heal blind eyes, remove diseases and pains in people's bodies, surely, he can give husbands.

It was this quest that led me on a journey to know the Holy Spirit, who he really was and how he wanted to make our lives comfortable (a comforter is to make our lives comfortable).

> *God said you will seek for him and find him when you search for him with all your heart* (Jeremiah 29:13) KJV

I began to practise his presence and walk with him. I began to hear his voice in small things like driving navigation. There were no satellite navigation aids in cars in those days, but I had the Holy Ghost who helped me many times when driving around the major highways of the US and Canada. It was during one of our fellowships together that He (the Holy Spirit) started prompting me to move out of Canada.

I hesitated initially as there was nothing in the natural that warranted a move; I had all that I desired, but I was single.

It seemed silly to the natural mind as I had everything working for me in Canada – a good job with a six-figure income, nice condo, nice car, nice friends, but He said to move back to England (I had emigrated to Canada from London 8 years earlier) and I obeyed with nothing backing that except a big promise and a big dream from a big God.

I relocated to London from Toronto with clearer directions from the Holy Spirit. He supernaturally made a way for me to move to London and get the required residence permits.

After seeking counsel with my dear praying friends, I made the move to the UK on October the 10th, six months after my thirty-sixth birthday.

I had to overcome several challenges including the loss of my purse on the journey to the airport, but it was miraculously posted to my address in England and to this day I don't know how the person found out my address.

CHAPTER 2

GOD IS PRO MARRIAGE

Our God the creator of heaven and earth, our Father is very pro-marriage, and He wants all that desire it to have it (Mark 11:24). This may be contrary to what some Christians believe and teach. It may even be contrary to your church doctrine. Some say that God is perfecting and pruning us by withholding from us, but there is no natural parent in their right mind that will want their 'thirty-something' year-old daughter or 'forty-something' year-old son to still be living at home with them and be single at that age.

The bible says if our earthly fathers that are 'wicked' know how to give good gifts, how much more our compassionate and loving heavenly Father?

> *'If you, then, though you are evil, know how to give good gifts to your children, how much more will your Father in heaven give good gifts to those who ask him'* Matthew 7:11 NIV

In the Old Testament, been single and unmarried was quite rare and unheard of amongst the Israelites. The unmarried were those who were outcasts by sicknesses and disease, those with exceptional or a divine call like Elijah, or those who had lost their spouses to death. All those who were old enough to be married were married, as it was in line with God's agenda in Genesis 1 & 2. Marriage was a norm in the Old Testament.

The first social event that our Lord Jesus attended while on earth was the marriage in Cana of Galilee (John 2:1-12). He did not only attend, he rescued them from shame. If he was not pro-marriage, why would he, the 'son of God', a man on a mission and with a vision on earth, waste his time attending a wedding and helping when they got stuck?

God is not schizophrenic or double-minded, he cannot say one thing and do the opposite, if he said it is NOT good that a man (or woman) be alone and then he will not act to the contrary.

All sickness, disease, poverty and lack are a work of the enemy. It happened because of the fall. Satan is the culprit that is responsible for all delay and the source of all your obstruction. God is a kind and a good God; the enemy's work was destroyed at redemption and God longs to give his children great and good gifts.

> *Every good gift and every perfect gift is from above, and cometh down from the Father of lights, with whom is no variableness, neither shadow of turning.* James 1:17 (KJV)

I strongly believe that God wants us to marry and have joy in marriage. I gleaned the following reasons from the bible:

Reason 1: He said it is not good for a man to be alone.

> *And the Lord God said, "It isn't good for man to be alone; I will make a companion for him, a helper suited to his needs."* Genesis 2:18 TLB

The most high, who made and manufactured us, crafted us for his glory said **it is not good**. If it is not good, then it is not his standard or his best intention. Man was made for companionship and needs a helper that is suited to his needs. You are an individual to God and not statistics. He wants you to be happy and settled in your home.

> *God settles the lonely in their homes.* Psalm 68:6a CEB

Reason 2: Marriage is honourable in all.

If God says marriage is honourable then it is a good thing to be desired. He wants all his children to have it when they desire it. It is precious to God as it is a replica of his relationship with the church. We are the bride of Christ. He wants our marriage relationships to represent the same.

> *Let marriage be held in honor (esteemed worthy, precious, of great price, and especially dear) in all things.* Hebrew 13:4a AMPC

> *The Amplified write that Marriage* is to be held *in honor among all [that is, regarded as something of great value]* Hebrew 13:4a AMP

Reason 3: Paul advocates that the younger women (widows) should re-marry.

Paul wrote more than half of the new testament. He was an authority in spiritual matters.

Surprisingly he did not advise they accept singleness as their lot in life or to busy themselves in the work of the Lord. If Paul who wrote more than half of the New Testament, God's mouthpiece and oracle advocated marriage to the younger widows, then the God he represents must be aligned to the same.

> *I desire therefore that the younger women marry, bear children, govern the house, giving no occasion to the adversary to speak reproachfully.* 1 Tim 5:14 JUB

Reason 4: Two are better than one.

Marriage relationship is to bring about lifelong friendship, companionship and partnership. God expects marriage to bring us advantages.

> *Two are better than one, because they have a good return for their labor:*

> *10 If either of them falls down, one can help the other up.*
> *But pity anyone who falls and has no one to help them up.*
> *11 Also, if two lie down together, they will keep warm.*
> *But how can one keep warm alone?*
> *12 Though one may be overpowered, two can defend themselves. A cord of three strands is not quickly broken.*
> Ecclesiastes 4:9-12 NIV

There are many advantages to being married to God's choice, the synergy factor is crucial in the race of life. Even the world recognises that two heads are better than one. You may be mighty in prayer alone but you can be mightier and more effective when you are two.

> *How should one chase a thousand, and two put ten thousand to flight. Deuteronomy 32:30a KJV.*

One of the most powerful prayers is the prayer of agreement between a husband and a wife.

Reason 5: To avoid fornication and self-gratification, God wants everyone to have their own spouse.

> *But because sexual immorality is so common each man should have his own wife, and each woman should have her own husband.* 1st Cor 7:2 HCSB

Reason 6: Marriage is established by God.

God himself instituted marriage, it is his ordination and he is the one that actually does the joining in marriage. It is a serious commitment. Therefore, it is a solemn promise not just to the spouse but before God. Divorce is not allowed except in a very limited number of biblically-prescribed circumstances. Jesus himself said they are no longer two separate people but one, and no man therefore must separate what God has joined together.

> *Have you not read that He who made[a] them at the beginning 'made them male and female,'[b] 5 and said, 'For this reason a man shall leave his father and mother and be joined to his wife, and the two shall become one flesh'?[c] 6 So then, they are no longer two but one flesh. Therefore, what God has joined together, let not man separate."*
> Matthew 19:4-6 (NKJV)

Reason 7: Procreation is only endorsed by God in a marriage.

Having children outside the marriage is not God's perfect plan, after he made Adam and Eve he blessed them and said to be fruitful and multiply.

> *So, God created man in His own image; in the image of God He created him; male and female He created them. 28 Then God blessed them, and God said to them, "Be fruitful and multiply; fill the earth and subdue it; have dominion over the fish of the sea, over the birds of the air, and over every living thing that moves on the earth." Genesis 1:27-29 KJV*

You are probably wondering why all the scriptures. I came to realise that God says what he means, and he means what he says. If he said explicitly that he desires for us to be married, then he has the power and the ability to back it up. His word is his bond, it is with these words that we make a case for our vindication.

The Many Phases a mature single goes through

1. 'Is he the one' Phase

Every single lady over the age of thirty who desires to be married will get to a stage where every single guy who walks into a room is under scrutiny and the question in your heart is 'is he the one?' Male platonic friendships at this age is even questionable as the ultimate question in the heart is 'will this lead to marriage?'

2. Desperation Phase

The age of thirty-five and over is quite critical, in that if your mind is not focused on God and you are not grounded in his love, you may start to waiver and to question the love of God for you. 'God if you do answer prayers, how come I have asked for a spouse for these many years and get no response?'

It is often at this stage that compromises set in and people lower their standards, and many will settle for unbelievers or anything in trousers.

3. Isolation Phase

Nearly forty? ...now what?

At this phase there is a temptation to isolate yourself and cut yourself off from friends and family and even the church. Anything in trousers (or skirts if you are a man) may seem to be the answer. You don't care anymore, anyone will do. This is a very dangerous phase where many will compromise and take whatever comes their way. It is understandable. Many have held on for two long and are weary of standing. People will give you unsolicited ungodly advices such as… Just have a child for anyone, be a mistress, God will forgive you if you commit adultery, he understands how long you have been waiting. Please don't listen to them, keep your focus on the Master.

4. Despondency

Nearly fifty… At this junction many have thrown in the towel and may even start getting bitter at God. You may even think it's too late. Complaining and griping is not the answer, and surely God has not abandoned or forsaken you. All sorts of suggestions will come from people who have given up on you. Suggestions as… Just adopt a child… nothing wrong with being a mistress to a man…

> 35 Therefore do not cast away your confidence, which has great reward. 36 For you have need of endurance, so that

after you have done the will of God, you may receive the promise:
37 For yet a little while, And He who is coming will come and will not tarry.
38 Now the just shall live by faith; But if anyone draws back, My soul has no pleasure in him.
39 But we are not of those who draw back to perdition, but of those who believe to the saving of the soul. God demands a level of confidence from us as a Christian. Hebrew 10:35-39 KJV

The bible says in 4 places that Christians are to live by faith. God loves us intensely and he urges us in verse 35 above not to put our confidence aside. Our confidence is a vital ingredient in prayer.

CHAPTER 3

SATAN'S LIES

Christians have an enemy, it is not your cousin, your aunty, your stepmother or your family member, those are only puppets in his hand. Our real enemy is the devil. He is a liar, deceiver and thief. He succeeded in deceiving Eve out of her inheritance and he still has many tricks and lies that he uses to deceive many out of their God-given inheritance.

> *He was a murderer from the beginning, and does not stand in the truth because there is no truth in him. When he lies, he speaks what is natural to him, for he is a liar and the father of lies and half-truths.* John 8:44B AMP

> *There is not an iota of truth in him. When he lies, it is perfectly normal; for he is the father of liars.* John 8:44 TLB

The devil is a proficient liar and I have highlighted some of the lies below. His intention is to keep people in their single state when they buy in to his lies.

1: God is preparing me.

God is preparing me… In my opinion this is the number one lie the enemy tells a lot of single Christian folks. This may be a true statement in some cases but for how long? How long will God need to prepare you? This is a grand deception of the devil; how long will it take for him to prepare you for a lifelong journey? Marriage is not a sprint, it is a marathon, a lifetime journey, you grow along the way with your spouse. God does not need to train you with lack or mature you until you are fifty before he gives you a spouse. It is all a lie, and married folks sometimes use this one on single people.

God is your maker, he knows your weakness and your strengths, and he knows how to connect you with the person that will complement you and bring out the best in you. You can NEVER be 100% perfect or ready for marriage, we are all in the growing process. Don't fall for this lie.

2: Maybe God has called me to be single.

If God called you to be single, you will not desire to marry. The fact that there is a desire in your heart for marriage clearly indicates you were not called to singleness. There is a grace from God to be single, this grace was upon our Lord Jesus, on John the Baptist and on Paul the Apostle for ministry, they were focused solely on their assignment. However, this grace of singleness was not on all the apostles. My understanding from the scriptures indicates that Peter and the other apostles were married.

> *Don't we have the right to bring a believing wife with us as the other apostles and the Lord's brothers do, and as Peter does?*
> 1 Corinthians 9:5 (NLT)

Even though the apostles were married they were all effective in their calling. Their marital status did not diminish their tenacity nor prevent them from carrying out their God-given mandate.

3: God time is the best.

As a mature single Christian, you will hear this phrase several times in many settings 'God's time is the best'. However almost every time you hear this phrase, you may begin to think God is the one that is withholding from you and even start to resent him on that basis. Why has he not released my provision? or why is he is delaying in the manifestation? This is all the deceit of the devil as God has already given. He is not the source of your lack.

God's patience is required when praying to be married but it is to be balanced with the 'NOW provision'. **God is a now God.** If you had a child that was sick would you ask that God take his time in healing him? No, you will want him (or her) healed right now. If you were sick in your body, it will be the same, you will want healing NOW. Jesus did not ask anyone to come back tomorrow, he heals all now. It is the same in praying for a spouse especially when you are overdue, God will not tell you to come back tomorrow. Your time is now.

The scriptures say there is a time for everything under the sun, there is a time to be single, a time to marry and a time to have a good family.

God refers to the 'wife of your youth' several times in the bible which indicates he expects marriage from the youth, not when one is old and grey. **God's time is NOW.** He has no hand in the delay that you are facing in the area of marriage, accepting that 'God's time is the best' is the trick of the enemy to make you accept the delay. If you believe God is the one behind your delay, you will not resist the enemy and you may stay without.

That verse 'God's time is the best' is not in the bible, it is an excuse from hell to keep you without the provision that God has for you.

> *There is a time for everything, and a season for every activity under the heavens.* Ecclesiastes 3:1. NIV

The writer of Ecclesiastes says there is a time for everything … there is a time to be single and a time to be married … When this timing is delayed and prolonged, the enemy is at work.

4: There is only one person created for me by God.

There is a myth that there is only one person God has created for you and that this person is your soul mate and he is the 'only' one for you. This is a lie from the enemy to keep a person looking for 'this one', who does not exist. This lie has kept some that were engaged or married to remain single after the relationship broke down. They think their soul mate was off with someone else and they were going to pray until he comes back. This is a lie to keep one in a state of singleness.

If you only had one soul mate. The question begs to be asked, what if you never meet this person before you reach the age of sixty? What if your paths never cross? What if he marries someone else?

Soul mates are not born. They're made. That's a fact that may discourage people who think marriage should be easy, but it's the truth. God created marriage to succeed. But that success requires us to put effort and energy into it. Good marriages require work.

God is too organized to be boxed into a corner, he is too detailed to yoke you with only 'one person' in the universe. In summary my 'loose' criteria for marriage are the following:

- Marry one who is a Christian
- Marry the opposite sex
- Marry one who is not married

5: I will marry an unbeliever and convert him.

Many singles have deceived themselves with this lie that it has become quite embarrassing. You are not the junior Holy Spirit, for He is the only person who can truly change a person's life.

Conversion is a personal conviction, it must happen before you commit to marry a person. Marrying an unbeliever is to have the devil as your father-in-law. It is better to be single than to marry the devil. No matter how cute or polished an unbeliever is, he is still hell bound until he accepts the intervention of Jesus. He or she is a cute devil unless they repent and accept the lordship of Jesus.

If one takes a pig and cleans it, manicures its nails and puts ribbons on its head and keeps him in a posh living room, he will be back in the mire in a short while. He will still return to dirt and the mire because that's its nature, it belongs there. The unbeliever has a nature of the devil, his father.

No matter how kind or charming he looks, he is from a different domain and you are not from the same kingdom.

6: This seems to be the major thing I pray about.

One of the lies of the devil is to make you believe that this is the only thing that you pray about, and God may not be pleased as 'souls are perishing'. Every sick person will continually pray to be healed and will seek all avenues to get well. Every unemployed person will channel all their energy into getting a job so why will a person who lacks a spouse not resist their lack with the same tenacity?

Abraham the 'father of faith' believed in God for a child and God counted it to him for righteousness. There is no record of him praying for anything else, he was a lover of God and he firmly believed that God would give him a child. He was not believing for anything else.

> *But Abram said, "Lord God, what will You give me, seeing I go childless, and the heir of my house is Eliezer of Damascus?"* Genesis 15:2 KJV

> *Abram said, "Lord [a]God, what* reward *will You give me, since I am [leaving this world] childless…* Genesis 15:2 TLB

There is absolutely nothing wrong in staking your claim to what rightfully belongs to you. This is your covenant right as a daughter/son of Abraham, so you have a right to it.

Some even say you have made this an idol, but this is a lie. You love God first and then claim your inheritance. Stake your claim with confidence.

7: There are more women than men in the world.

This is another grand lie, God made you, you are so special, and he made you the right gender, with a purpose. He made every female to be wife to a man and every male a husband to a woman. Jesus in the book of John 15:16a (AMP) said:

> *You have not chosen me, but I have chosen you and I have appointed and placed and purposefully planted you...*
> John 15:16a AMP

Your life is planned, you are not a biological accident or a product of just a man and a woman sleeping together. You are a creature on appointment. Destiny is at work in you. God has all our life planned to the finest details.

8: There are no men in my church.

This is what many short-sighted believers say and how they reason. They think they must be in a church full of the opposite sex to get a spouse. Lie, Lie, Lie… Your husband does not have to be in your church or be a member of the church. It is a cult that would expect you to marry ONLY someone from your denomination. The body of Christ is bigger than your church.

God is the ultimate matchmaker, he can make it happen regardless of your location. He knows where you are, and he will connect you. The Holy Spirit the 'champion connector' is the one you need to get a spouse. He will navigate you to your provision.

I know the testimony of a friend who went to school in a village in Nova Scotia Canada and met her spouse there. Who goes to school in such an obscure place and finds a spouse? But God planted her provision there even before she got there. I know another who went to school in Wisconsin and found her husband there.

To conclude, you do not go to church to get a man. Amongst other things you go to church to get the **Word** to get a man. The word can 'Manufacture' anything. You need to love God for who he is, knowing he loves you and has a plan for your life.

9: God is trying to teach me and train me.

God does not teach us with lack. This is a lie of the devil. No natural parent will train their child with sickness, disease or lack. He has made the five-fold ministry available to teach and train his children.

> Ephesians 4:11-12
>
> *And he gave some, apostles; and some, prophets; and some, evangelists; and some, pastors and teachers;*
>
> *12* **For the perfecting of the saints**, *for the work of the ministry, for the edifying of the body of Christ:*

God does not perfect his children with lack, affliction or want. He lets the word do that. He is not the one withholding from you. He has already made available to us all things that pertain to this life and godliness.

10: I am too old.

God knows your age, he knows your biological clock is ticking and you do not need to convince him with your crying or mental gymnastics.

He has a provision for you regardless of your age. 24 or 64, he can make it happen. No one is too old to marry if they are ready for marriage.

In addition to the above, I will need to clarify the following which may be more prevalent in some specific parts of the globe.

Same sex marriage
The promotion of diversity in the Western world has been to make it embrace all types of atrocities and make light of this sin.

Everything that is an abomination to God seems to have been embraced and legalized in the Western world, but human legislation does not mean God's endorsement.

Marriage is not merely a civil union and human agreement between two consenting individuals i.e. male and female. It is a living and active relationship before and under God (Genesis 2:22). So even in this dispensation of grace, God will only sanction a marriage between a male and a female.

Polygamy

In some parts of the world, Polygamy is acceptable, and a man can have more than one wife at the same time, but what is acceptable to man may not be acceptable to God. A Christian woman MUST never compromise as to be a second wife to a man. A Christian man MUST not have more than one wife. God will not endorse such a marriage. Three times in the scripture Paul admonished the deacons (anyone who serves in any leadership capacity) to be the husband of ONLY one wife

> *² A bishop then must be blameless, the husband of one wife, vigilant, sober, of good behaviour, given to hospitality, apt to teach;* 1 Timothy 3:2(KJV)

> *¹² Let the deacons be the husbands of one wife, ruling their children and their own houses well.* 1 Timothy 3:2& 12(KJV)

> *⁵ I left you in Crete to do what still needed to be done – appointing spiritual leaders[a] in every city as I directed you. ⁶ A spiritual leader must have a good reputation. He must have **only one wife** and have children who are believers. His children shouldn't be known for having wild lifestyles or being rebellious'* Titus 1:5-7(NOG)

CHAPTER 4

THE FAVOUR FACTOR

God loves you intensely and only he can love you completely, there is no human being on this earth that can love you the way he loves you. Romantic novels mislead people on the issue of love, this is all fantasy and this love is unrealistic. God is the best lover, trust him completely. Your desire for God must exceed your desire for anything else including a spouse.

In this chapter, I want to state that an understanding of the love of God for us is liberating. Paul prayed that we may know the love of God that passes knowledge (Ephesians 3:19 KJV).

This knowledge of this love is an antidote for inadequacies. Most ladies struggle with inadequacies… not slim enough, not tall enough, not fair enough, not pretty enough, not elegant, not curvy enough… we are all fearfully and wonderfully made; some more fearfully than others.

There will always be someone who is better, finer, prettier… than you in one way or the other but in my own research, the most significant requirement for getting a spouse is not beauty, it's not the 'guitar' figure eight, it's not the perfect pout, not the perfect height, it is FAVOUR. Favour is a big word and one of the biggest keys to getting a spouse. His love procured favour for us.

Favour is powerful. Favour determines the limit of every man's destiny. Favour is what separates the girlfriends from the wives. It is what makes a man choose one, even though he has many options. No human being can rise higher than the favour of God upon their life.

The preacher saw this and wrote

> *I returned, and saw under the sun, that the race is not to the swift, nor the battle to the strong, neither yet bread to the wise, nor yet riches to men of understanding, nor yet favour to men of skill; but time and chance happeneth to them all.*
> Ecclesiastes 9:11 (KJV)

Marriage is a function of favour, not just good looks. If marriage was just based on good looks, every beautiful lady will be married, and every handsome man will have a beautiful wife. Have you sometimes wondered why a 'not-too-good-looking lady' can land a fantastic guy and vice versa? You cannot seem to figure it out.

The dictionary defines favour as endorsement, approval, support, or liking for someone or something. It is an act of kindness beyond what is due or usual. It is synonymous with approval, approbation, commendation, esteem, goodwill, kindness, benevolence and friendliness.

Looking good is important and thank God for Mary Kay, MAC and Maybelline, L'Oréal – they do help people to look good but the best of all is FOG (favour of God).

Jesus had to grow in favour and with man, Luke 2:52 (KJV)), if Jesus who had the Spirit without measure needed to grow in favour, then we need to do the same.

Finding a godly spouse has little to do with your age, looks, income, race etc. If this was the case, everyone with these attributes will be happily married. Looking sharp is great and dressing well is good but it is not the primary requirement for marriage. Have you not seen the blind marry? The deaf and the mute marry? The disabled marry? So why will an able-bodied believer with two eyes, two legs and a good job remain single?

Favour is the key. Favour does the following:

I. Favour opens every man's future. Every destiny is limited by its access to favour. Favour turns captives to captain.
II. Favour is greater than hard work.

> *Lord, by Your favour You had set me strong as a mountain Psalm 30:7 (MEV)*

> *So then [it is] not of him that wills, nor of him that runs, but of God that shews ... Romans 9:16 (NLT)*

III. Favour is superior to strength.

> *For by strength shall no man prevail.* 1st Sam 2:9 (KJV).

IV. Favour is preferential treatment. Favour endorses us and make one stand above all others.
V. Favour brings us to a place of prominence. see Genesis 30:4
VI. Favour enables requests to be granted Exodus. see12:36

> *And Jesus increased in wisdom and stature, and in favour with God and man.* (Luke 2:52)

> If Jesus had to increase in favour then we need to increase as well.

VII. Favour translates to 'Grace' in many languages, Paul admonishes that this Grace can be multiplied through the full absolute knowledge of the word of God. I pray that you receive multiplied grace for marriage now!
VIII. Favour makes one possess their inheritance. See Psalm 44:3

It is favour that causes a man to propose to a woman and to prefer her above all other women. God will give you special preference for marriage as you read now.

Esther's story

The story of Esther is such a powerful analogy; this lady was an orphan, an immigrant, probably had an accent and was unschooled in the ways of the Persians. She had no natural advantages and was not polished; her guardian was a porter, he was to be seen and not heard.

There are several mentions of favour in this story to buttress my conviction that favour was key factor to her landing in the king's palace. This lady, who was to replace Vashti, started by finding favour with their custodian. (Please read the whole story of her selection as Queen in the first two chapters of the book of Esther.)

> *Now the young woman pleased Hegai and found **favor** with him. So he quickly provided her with beauty preparations and her [portion of] food, and he gave her seven choice maids from the king's palace; then he transferred her and her maids to the best place in the harem.* Esther 2:9 (AMP)

In verse 15, Hegai gave her tips to win the king's heart. The bible does not record him doing so for the other virgins. She was given insider information.

> *When it was Esther's turn to go to the king, she accepted the advice of Hegai, the eunuch in charge of the harem, dressing according to his instructions;* Esther 2:15A TLB
> *And Esther obtained favor in the sight of all who saw her* Esther 2:15B NKJV

This woman was irresistible, all that looked upon her favoured her, and finally the same spirit of preference caused her to be chosen. She was not the most beautiful, as the bible records that all the other virgins were all beautiful. Secondly, they all had the same beauty therapies and treatments, thirdly they were cared for and nurtured by the same coordinators, but this favour made her to stand out of all the virgins, Esther was chosen as Queen. The 'FOG' was at work.

> *Now the king loved Esther more than all the other women, and she found **favor** and kindness with him more than all*

> the [other] virgins, so that he set the royal crown on her head and made her queen in the place of Vashti. Esther 2:17 TLB

The key word in this passage is that she found favour more than all the other virgins that the king chose her. This favour is still at work today to give you, the reader, favour where you need it most.

Ruth The Moabite
This favour was upon Ruth, an outcast, a foreigner and a widow. Her tribe originated from Moab, the Jews did not reckon with them. They were a lineage tainted with incest but the 'FOG' was at work and she got the most eligible bachelor of her time, Boaz.

Rachel, Jacob's wife
Jacob was willing to serve his dubious father-in-law for a total of fourteen years for Rachel. He got Leah, but she was not good enough. The favour of God on Rachel's life was so strong it empowered Jacob to work for seven more years to marry her.

Favour Confessions
Now make these confessions:

> In the name of Jesus, I speak that I am known and loved by God, I have a right standing with him and I am the righteousness of God. Therefore, I have a right to his covenant of peace, kindness and favour.
>
> God surrounds 'me', the righteous as a shield with favour. Therefore, the FOG surrounds me everywhere I go and in everything I do. I expect the favour of God to be in full manifestation in every area of my life and on every occasion. This favour causes me to be preferred and located for marriage.
>
> The favour of God upon my life is like a magnet, it attracts my God ordained provision to me.

I will never be without the favour of God again. This FOG is like a cloak, it covers me and rests richly upon me. It abundantly abounds in me. Every anti-favour mark has been washed away by the blood of Jesus, and I am now experiencing God's favour immeasurably, abundantly, limitlessly, and exceedingly.

Please make time to make these confessions daily.

CHAPTER 5

YOUR SPIRITUAL NETWORK MATTERS

Christianity in itself is a matter of discovery. Discovering what Jesus has paid for and possessing it. Ignorance is not bliss in Christianity. We must understand the rules of engagement and play by these rules.

In my research I found out it was possible to be anointed and be single, just like it is possible to be anointed and be sick or broke or even die. All afflictions are sponsored by the same enemy.

The mission of the Holy Spirit.
The Christian is the most powerful of God's creation. He was created to rule and to have dominion (Psalm 8). This is a privilege and a responsibility for which we must answer.

When Jesus was on earth, he was limited to a geographical location. He was not omnipresent, he could not be everywhere at the same time. He could only commute between the cities surrounding Nazareth BUT when he was leaving for heaven he gave us (the Christian) the Holy Spirit. The Holy Spirit is not a feeling or just speaking in tongues, he is the most significant personality on planet earth today. He is here to help us live a successful Christian life. The Holy Spirit in the Christian makes him undefeatable.

I write more about his ministry in chapter nine.

Which Church are you planted in?
Your church matters. Some churches do not celebrate marriage. In these churches the married live like they are single and there is no great emphasis on marriage. Married couples often minister separately and can even pastor separate churches. These churches often have a lot of singletons especially among the women, and the single men may go outside the church to marry and bring their spouses in. There are many single leaders in such churches (especially women).

Where marriage is not celebrated or preached there will be no marriages. Where the pastor does not spend time praying for his spiritual daughters to be married they will remain single.

> Mark 11:23 (KJV) says we will have whatsoever we say and the word also states:
>
> *Say unto them, as truly as I live, saith the Lord, as ye have spoken in mine ears, so will I do to you.* Numbers 14:28 (KJV)

As a mature single you need to be planted in a church (not multiple churches) where the preached word is alive. As an active member of a church you can be held accountable and not fall prey to sexual sins.

There are some selfish pastors who insist that a woman needs to get a spouse within the church (even where there are only a handful of single men in the church) and such pastors control the lives of these ladies. That's a destructive pastor, especially since he has a wife of his own. If your pastor is not committed to your getting a spouse, you may need to relocate and look for a pastor that wants it well with you.

It is good to be planted in a church that believes in the vision of marriage, a church that does not pray for the singles to be married will not see marriages.

When I was believing to be married, my pastors were great supporters both emotionally and spiritually. I will forever be grateful to God for their lives.

Who are you listening to?
Who are the people that speak into your life? These people can make or break you. Listening to good counsel is very important for mature Christians.

> *For by wise counsel thou shalt make thy war: and in multitude of counsellors there is safety.* Prov 24:6 KJV.

People that speak into your life will see what you do not see. You may be clouded by emotions and overlook some significant details. They will be your eyes and will see beyond the pretty face.

Where are you located?
Location, Location, Location – you've probably heard this in relation to properties, but this is very relevant in getting a God-ordained spouse.

In Genesis 24 1– end, There is a profound story that the Holy spirit has chosen to document in a whole chapter. It is how the Holy spirit helps to get a spouse.

Abraham sent his chief servant to get a wife for his only son. This was a very difficult task as Abraham trusted the God of heaven to send an angel to help his servant to make the right choice for his heir.

> *The* Lord *God of heaven, which took me from my father's house, and from the land of my kindred, and which spake unto me, and that sware unto me, saying, Unto thy seed will I give this land; he shall send his angel before thee, and thou shalt take a wife unto my son from thence* Genesis 24:7 KJV

His servant (probably Eliezer) prayed and asked God's help.

> *And he said O Lord God of my master Abraham, I pray thee, send me good speed this day, and shew kindness unto my master Abraham.*
> *13 Behold, I stand here by the well of water; and the daughters of the men of the city come out to draw water:*

14 And let it come to pass, that the damsel to whom I shall say, Let down thy pitcher, I pray thee, that I may drink; and she shall say, Drink, and I will give thy camels drink also: let the same be she that thou hast appointed for thy servant Isaac; and thereby shall I know that thou hast shewed kindness unto my master.
15 And it came to pass, before he had done speaking, that, behold, Rebekah came out, who was born to Bethuel, son of Milcah, the wife of Nahor, Abraham's brother, with her pitcher upon her shoulder. Genesis 24:13-15 KJV

God is amazing, he does not just position the ordained wife in the set location/position that the servant specified in prayer. He (God) also ensured that she was from the race specified by Abraham … detailed enough to even be a relative.

This implies that there is someone assigned (a member of the Christian family) for you in a 'particular' place.

Now pray for divine positioning that you will be in the right place at the right time. Speak that you are walking in prepared paths and that your steps will be ordered by God.

CHAPTER 6

GET RID OF BLOCKERS

Hindrances #1: False and unrealistic expectation
Many are looking for what does not exist, these people only exist in their bubble or better still a pipe dream. It is a figment of their imagination. Ladies want a six-footer, handsome, a millionaire, who drives a lovely car, has a mansion, with a well-established professional job and who knows their thoughts even before they articulate such… and the list goes on.

Men likewise are looking for a pretty, fair-skinned, slim but guitar-shaped woman, with the best pout and who will not challenge them in any way, intelligent but completely submissive and looks up to them, someone who can massage their fragile egos.

These are false expectations, if you see anything that seems too good to be true then it really is not true. If you see any man that is all made up and done, he probably belongs to someone else. Believe God for your own and get ready to polish and tidy him/her up.

Hindrances #2: Do not be side-tracked by the wrapper – it is only used for packaging.
Many that desire a spouse often look at natural things. Please note that looks are quite important, but it should not be the highest on your priority list. The reason for this is that looks are never the ultimate. Looks are deceptive, a cute-looking guy may be a loser or a free loader. A beautiful

lady may not always be the most generous and may not look that great when the makeup is off. Looks are temporary, you cannot base a lasting relationship on it.

> *Charm can be deceptive, and beauty doesn't last, but a woman who fears and reverences God shall be greatly praised.*
> Proverbs 31(MSG)

A lot of the romantic novels have skewed the mentality of many ladies. So, they are looking for a handsome man with broad shoulders, who will take them for romantic dinners, buy them flowers and loads of gifts.

In 1 Samuel 16, the prophet Samuel was looking for a new king and the Lord sent him to Jesse's house. Jesse had a house full of sons, he had eight sons. So, it could be any of them. Even the prophet Samuel (as anointed as he was then) was nearly deceived; he looked at Eliab and he had the correct stature and gravitas, he looked and spoke well. The appropriate physique, carriage and charisma for the throne BUT the Lord refused him.

> *So it was, when they came, that he looked at Eliab and said, "Surely the Lord's anointed is before Him!"*
> *But the Lord said to Samuel, "Do not look at his appearance or at his physical stature, because I have refused him. For the Lord does not see as man sees; [a] for man looks at the outward appearance, but the Lord looks at the heart."* 1 Samuel 16:6-7 (KJV)

This is a great lesson not to observe the packaging. Eliab had the right packaging and physical appearance, but he lacked God's approval. A packaging is only a wrapper, it will be silly for a person to choose or assess the value of a gift based on its beautiful wrapper.

In my opinion this is one of the biggest hindrances of most ladies. Do not be moved only by his looks or his job or his car. Most are looking for a 'ready-made' man. Check out what is in the heart.

Hindrances #3: Rigidity about how I must meet my spouse

Some people still believe that the only place they can meet their intended spouse is in church or in a religious gathering. This is a misconception as the Holy Spirit moves in diverse ways. You intended spouse does not have to be a member of your church. The biblical criteria for getting married is for him to be a believer. If you both believe the bible as the highest authority and are both teachable, you will succeed in marriage.

Introduction and matchmaking:

Do not be rigid about the way you want to meet your spouse, rigidity will hinder the work of the Holy Spirit who is the perfect matchmaker.

The Holy Spirit told me while waiting that I was only **one person away from my husband**. i.e. there is one person who knows you and knows your intended spouse and he, the Holy Spirit, can quicken that person to remember you.

Some ladies do not like to be introduced, they believe the meeting must be spontaneous as in a romantic novel … this is what the romantic novels postulate but may not always be the case. Introduction to a person and matchmaking is actually scriptural, (Naomi introduced Ruth to Boaz and did all the matchmaking) and there is absolutely nothing wrong with it. Don't let your perspective delay your miracle.

Perspective on Social Networks, Dating agencies:

In this digital age, everything that you need is probably a website away. I am not the biggest fan of internet dating or web dating apps, but you cannot put God in a strait jacket. There are Christian ladies who have met their Christian husbands through internet dating and who are happily married. Let God lead you and proceed accordingly.

Regardless of whichever way you meet the intended spouse, you will still need to do your own due diligence. Even if he is a bishop, you need to check him out, find out his background, his family, his friends, and his character etc.

When you are meeting someone for the first time, meet them in a neutral place and not in their homes or a private/secluded place. Use your brain and don't let your desire to be married cloud your initiative and thinking.

And as in Tracy's testimony below, there is no right or wrong way to meet your spouse.

Hindrances #4: Holding on to the past
Holding on to the past can hinder the plan God has for your life now. The past is history and needs to be buried. Please let Saul go so that the 'David' God has anointed for you can emerge.

> *Remember not the former things, nor consider the things of old.*
> *19 Behold, I am doing a new thing; now it springs forth, do you not perceive it? I will make a way in the wilderness and rivers in the desert.* Isaiah 43:18-19 ESV

Every partner that did not marry you was God delivering you from a heartache, it was not a loss, it was God's hand navigating to your own provision. Let the past be in the tomb and tomorrow in the womb.

Let go of the past and some blaming yourself or anyone else. It was not your fault. Your own will not pass you by.

Hindrances # 5: Accomplishment before marriage
This is especially true amongst men, they desire to succeed in many areas before they are married. Success for them is measured by accumulation of natural things. i.e. build/buy their own home, establish and grow their own business, have several employees and several cars. All these are nice to have but are not prerequisites for a great marriage. Do not despise the days of small beginnings.

> *Then, even if your beginnings were modest, your final days will be full of prosperity.* Job 8:7 CSB

> *Those who have made fun of this day of small beginnings will celebrate when they see Zerubbabel holding this important stone* Zechariah 4:10a CEV

Hindrances # 6: Fear of Commitment

This is also relatively prevalent amongst men, the fear of committing to one woman. One of the questions that the enemy poses is 'what if she is not the right person?' A lot go through so many options and may eventually settle for that which may not necessarily be the best. As a Christian, we are to trust God and acknowledge him in our choices. An understanding of the love of God will drive out all fear. God loves us too much to let us make mistakes. For a Christian there is nothing to fear. Fear is a magnet for the adversary to afflict, just like faith is a magnet for God to create and bless.

> *Don't be afraid. I am with you. Don't tremble with fear. I am your God.*
> *I will make you strong, as I protect you with my arm.* Isaiah 41:10

CHAPTER 7

THOSE YOU SHOULD NOT DATE OR MARRY

1. An unbeliever: There is no future in connecting with an unbeliever no matter how cute his is, if he is not a Christian he has the devil as his father. Marrying him will only end in heartbreak and a long journey of compromise and frustration.

   Many have made the mistake of thinking they will convert him. The only person that can convert a human being is the Holy Ghost and since you are not the junior Holy Ghost, this is not on your job spec. If he is not saved before he marries, the probability that he will be saved afterwards is remote. Resist this temptation and choose to wait for the one God has for you.

   > *Do not be yoked together with unbelievers. For what do righteousness and wickedness have in common? Or what fellowship can light have with darkness?*
   > 2 Corinthians 6:14 (NIV)

   Don't be too desperate to compromise. Whatever you compromise to keep, you will eventually lose.

2. An unbelieving believer: These are lukewarm Christians. They take the word and the things of God lightly. These are unteachable Christians. They are not committed to the things

of God and those who are committed are labelled fanatics. These people think church is a social gathering and a place to make connections.

> *I know your deeds, that you are neither cold nor hot. I wish you were either one or the other! So, because you are lukewarm—neither hot nor cold—I am. ... that you are neither cold nor hot. I wish you were either one or the other! 16 So, because you are lukewarm—neither hot nor cold—I am about to spit you out of my mouth* Rev 3:15-16 (NIV)

3. A believer who has no reverential fear of God: These are worse than unbelievers. They make light of sin and have no 'fear' of God. They are like the sons of Samuel, close to the anointing but making light of the things of the spirit. Adultery is 'no big deal' and purity is outdated. They have no reverence for God or church authority. He will talk you into in a compromising position that you may regret.

4. A smooth operator: He does the talk but does not walk the walk. He talks about God and he appears deep, he's always hanging around you, but he never really makes a commitment to you.

   Everyone knows he is close to you and thinks you are an item but he 'feigns' ignorance of this. Talk is cheap. Some of them even use the excuse of a 'broken heart' as the reason for their actions and can even ask that you keep it a secret away from the pastor. Just a relationship between 'both of us'. Anyone that is not proud to be seen with you has a hidden agenda, let him go so he does not spoil your chances with the serious one.

5. The angry guy: He gets angry and does not have control over his temper or speech. He is like a volcano waiting to erupt. He gets angry and spills his guts. He has a short fuse and can embarrass you at the drop of a hat. Get rid of him quickly.

> *Make no friendship with an **angry man**, and with a furious **man** do not go* Proverbs 22:24 (KJV)

> *Don't hang out with angry people; don't keep company with hotheads. Bad temper is contagious, don't get infected Proverbs 22:25 MSG*

6. The struggling person: He is always on his way and never overcomes. Struggles to keep time, struggling to be accountable to anyone, never has his finances in control. Always going through but never coming out. In my own words he is a scatterbrain… Always going through something. He is the needy type. Walk away from him.

7. Obsessive guys: These are guys who will choke you in a relationship; he is a leech and you cannot turn anywhere without him knowing where you are at any point in time. It is okay for a person to be wanted but there is a balance. This type of person wants to micro-manage you and he says he will end his life when you are not in it. Use wisdom to detach yourself from this type of person.

8. Sexually-driven guys: Anyone who pressures you to sleep with him before he marries you is not worthy of you. Sexual sin will cripple your walk with God and leave you with a guilty conscience, unwanted pregnancy or a sexually transmitted disease. Don't be in a hurry, wait until your honeymoon. Why buy the cow when you can have the milk for free? Run away from this type of person.

> *Run from sexual sin! No other sin so clearly affects the body as this one does. For sexual immorality is a sin against your own body.* 1 Corinthians 6:18 (NLT)

9. The one who never commits: These are commitment phobia guys. He hangs out with you and drops innuendos but never actually commits himself to you. He is a time-waster, he is not going anywhere. He hangs around all the beautiful ladies

and is affectionate to all but does not commit to any. He will break your heart. Walk away from such a man. These ones are skilful at manipulating people and are clever at coning the opposite sex. They often lead the opposite sex on without making a commitment. They use insinuations that can easily be misinterpreted by a lonely heart and are experts at stringing many ladies along.

10. A man without a vision: A man without a vision has no purpose in life, he only lives for the now and does not see or plan for tomorrow. He is blind and cannot see beyond his nose. A person with a vision is better than a person with money. Money can be temporary, but a visionary can create wealth and multiple streams of income.

> *Where there is no vision [no redemptive revelation of God], the people perish;* Proverbs 19:18a AMPC

A dictionary definition of vision is the ability to think about or plan the future with imagination or wisdom. It is synonymous with creativity, creative power, inventiveness, innovation, inspiration, intuition, perceptiveness, foresight, insight, far-sightedness, and discernment. These are critical building blocks in a marriage and for a long-term relationship.

11. A flippant man: These ones talk out of turn and are careless talkers. They are always talking and putting other people down. Anointed critics and professional fault finders. These cannot bridle their tongue. They are foolish men and will get you both in trouble. Nabal, was such a man in the bible and his beautiful and intelligent wife was Abigail; I often wonder why she married a foolish man.

> *The man's name was Nabal, and his wife's name was Abigail. She was an intelligent and attractive woman, but her husband was a hard man who did evil things. He was a Calebite.* 1st Samuel 25:3 CEB

> *Let not my lord, I pray you, regard this foolish and wicked fellow Nabal, for as his name is, so is he— Nabal [foolish, wicked] is his name, and folly is with him.* 1st Samuel 25:25 AMPC

12. The lazy guy: There are many around these days. They are allergic to work and will look for a wife who can bear the load, while they live a stress-free life. If he does not have a job (no matter how small) he does not have a business looking for a wife. He is a free loader.

CHAPTER 8

MAXIMISE YOUR LIFE

Singleness is only a season of life and just like a natural season cannot last forever; even so this season like any natural season is temporary, it will not last forever, it is subject to change. No matter how dark it is at night there must be a dawn. No matter how bad a winter it is, it must give way to spring. Seasons are transient, they last for a short period of time.

> *Weeping may endure for a night, but joy comes in the morning.* Psalm 30:5 KJV

This is a temporal season, so you cannot make permanent decisions around this season. You cannot afford to give up and settle for anything less than God's best.

Here are some tips to help maximise your life and live it to the fullest before you marry.

Tip # 1: Develop an intimacy with God.

> When one is single one can commit to spending quality time with God whenever you want. There are no distractions and like Paul wrote to the Corinthian church, it's a time where you can give your "undivided devotion to the Lord" (1 Corinthians 7:35). Therefore, devote yourself to knowing God by hearing the preached word (especially

about God's providing ability), studying, and spending time in praise and worship.

Establish and deepen your relationship with God, not use church activities as a crutch but as an avenue to express your love for God. Let God define who you are not your job, or family or history, or circumstances. Let the past stay in the past. Agree with God and what he said about you. You are what God says you are. Embrace his love and do not take it for granted. His love for us is unconditional, not based on performance.

While waiting on God for my provision, I spent a lot of time in the word and a minimum of an hour on Saturdays dancing and rejoicing before the Lord. I called it 'Jamming for the Lamb', I still engage in this to this day; however, it is not as regimented as it used to be before I was married. So please make the most of this time that you are single.

Tip # 2: Serve God Diligently.

During this season you should make the most of your life naturally and spiritually. You should serve God with all your might and strength. When I was believing to be married, I was not just diligent in church I was nicknamed the 'mother of the church'. I was one of the first in and the last to leave. I was most committed at events and conferences; my anchor theme at this time was that God is a righteous rewarder, he does not only reward those that seek him but they that seek him diligently. He has not called the seed of Jacob to seek him in vain.

Service gets God's attention. Anna served God in the temple with fasting and God qualified her to see the Messiah. Serve with passion. Use your gifts and talents to bring him glory.

Tip # 3 Connect and make vital relationships.

Connecting and making vital and progressive relationships are important at this point of your life. Link up with people that can mentor you and speak into your life. Please note that you may notice obvious weaknesses in mentors as you get closer to them, please don't let this put you off. People that God designed to speak into your life are also human. Wisdom and discernment is important on your part so as not to overlook the people God has sent to you.

These vital relationships are also destiny helpers. I invested in quality friendships and surrounded myself with rewarding relationships and alliances which eventually paid off and connected me to my provision. All these mentors and alliances still play a significant role in my life today.

In the Testimonies below, it was such a relationship that helped secure their provision.

Being single doesn't mean being alone. No man is an island and a tree does not make a forest. Get wisdom and get connected.

> *24 And let us consider how we may spur one another on toward love and good deeds, 25 not giving up meeting together, as some are in the habit of doing, but encouraging one another – and all the more as you see the Day approaching.* Hebrews 10:24-25(NIV)

When you become a Christian, you immediately become a part of the body of Christ and a member of his family as well. And in this family, you have been called both to encourage and be an encourager. Your testimony is closer than you think.

Pray that God will connect you to destiny helpers.

Tip # 4: Commit to keeping yourself pure.

You may wonder, how can I keep myself pure in this sexually-driven age? The internet, TV, magazines, adverts on billboards and posters all have sexual innuendos and undertones. These all seem harmless and natural to the world. Living together before marriage and sex outside marriage is accepted in the world but not to God. Fornication, adultery, homosexuality, pornography and all sexual immorality is still a sin before God. Paul tells us to flee from sexual immorality. The word flee literally means to run away in terror, just like we will run when we see a rattle snake or an explosive device.

> *17 But he who is joined to the Lord is one spirit with Him.*
> *18 Flee sexual immorality. Every sin that a man does is outside the body, but he who commits sexual immorality sins against his own body.*
> *19 Or do you not know that your body is the temple of the Holy Spirit who is in you, whom you have from God, and you are not your own?*
> 1 Corinthians 6:17-19 (NKJV)

Sexual contacts outside God's design is destructive, it cuts short and cuts off a destiny. Samson is a good example from the word. He let his sex drive destroy his glorious calling (he had an anointing of might). Paul wrote to Timothy:

> *Flee also youthful lusts: but follow righteousness*
> 2 Timothy 2:22 KJV

Tip # 5 Financial Investment towards your future.

When one is single there is tendency to want to indulge in excesses: designer labels, multiple shoes, clothes etc. This is okay if you can afford it, but it is also a great time to start investing. Stop renting and buy or build your own house. Invest for your future and your retirement. The funding that you have readily available now may need to be diverted to the children when married, so it's a smart move to invest now.

Tip # 6 Get to know yourself.

This season of singleness is valuable and precious time that can be used to really get to know and love yourself; if you are not comfortable with yourself you cannot be comfortable with someone else. So, spend the time getting to know yourself. What are the areas of your life that can be improved? Can someone live with me and be comfortable? Am I selfless enough to overlook a fault? When married you no longer have your own space, you cannot escape from this person.

Tip # 7 Don't put your life on hold. Enjoy yourself.

Don't just park your life because your spouse has not yet manifested. Do what you need to do and enjoy yourself. Travel and visit exotic places. Learn a new language, join a gym or a start a new craft. Do not hibernate or cut yourself off but recognise that this period will be over shortly.

In my season of singleness, I travelled extensively, mostly with my friends (and thanks also to my consulting job). I visited countries in North and South America, Africa, Europe and Asia. I joined Zumba classes and improved on my Spanish. All these pay off.

CHAPTER 9

Pray, Pray and Pray

Prayer is the biggest ingredient in the mix of getting married as a mature single. You cannot 'over pray' and there is no overdose in praying but you must be praying aright.

John Wesley, founder of the Methodist Church said, "It seems like God is limited by our prayer life. He can do nothing for humanity unless someone asks Him to do it."

Unanswered prayers erode our confidence but a knowledge of our right standing with God is a springboard for answered prayers. Our right standing with God is not our feelings, performance or history. It is not based on what we have done or can ever do. It is based on the blood that Jesus shed for us. Righteousness (or right standing)with God is a free gift. This is what qualifies us for answered prayers.

> *For if by the one man's offense death reigned through the one, much more those who receive abundance of grace and **of the gift of righteousness** will reign in life through the One, Jesus Christ.* Romans 5:17 NKJV

The footnotes of the living bible 'kings of life', literally mean "reign in life".

God answers prayer, he does not postpone or defer prayers. He has the ability and capacity to answer and always answers.

> *O You Who hear prayer, to You shall all flesh come.*
> Psalm 65:2 AMPC

As a mature single you must understand the following:

1. God is not withholding from you, he is a generous giver.
   He loves you more than any natural parent can love a child and he has great plans for your life. He is the source of every good gift. (James 1:17) and has given all things that pertain to your life and for you to live a great life on earth. He has great plans for your life.

   > *The Lord has appeared of old to me, saying: "Yes, I have loved you with an everlasting love; Therefore, with loving kindness I have drawn you."*
   > Jeremiah 31:3 NKJV

2. God is not your problem, or the source of your challenge and he will never cause you pain or harm you.
   Jesus Christ was sent to die to terminate the works of the devil.

   > *The reason the Son of God was made manifest (visible) was to undo (destroy, loosen, and dissolve) the works the devil [has done]* 1 John 3:8b AMPC

3. God is not the cause of your delay or trying to teach you a lesson. (Refer to the section above where we address the lies of the devil.)
   God is not confused or double-minded. He cannot put something on you and require that you prayed to him to remove it.

4. The source of all opposition, hindrances and delay is the devil.
   It is not your aunty, cousin or relative, those are just instruments he used. The grand master is the devil.

> *Because it was our will to come to you. [I mean that] I, Paul, again and again [wanted to come], but **Satan hindered** and impeded us.*
> 1 Thessalonians 2:18 AMPC

> *Be sober, be vigilant; because your adversary the devil...* 1 Peter 5:8a KJV

5. The good news is that you have the God-given ability and the delegated power to bring about a change in your situation (Luke 10:19). God has given us the divine ability to bring about changes.

   > *Awake, awake; put on thy strength, O Zion; put on thy beautiful garments, O Jerusalem, the holy city: for henceforth there shall no more come into thee the uncircumcised and the unclean.*
   > *Shake thyself from the dust; arise, and sit down, O Jerusalem: loose thyself from the bands of thy neck, O captive daughter of Zion.* Isaiah 52:1& 2 KJV

6. You will need to select and fully understand the scriptures you are standing on.

   Faith and prayer goes together, so you need to ensure you have faith for the area you are praying for.

   Faith always comes by hearing the word of God, (Romans 10:17). Either the word is preached to you or you speak it to yourself in confessions. Get some scripture to stand on and speak out, I have listed some scriptures above in chapter 2.

   David chose five smooth stones to defeat his goliath. He only needed to use one. Jesus spoke against the devil and said, 'it is written' three separate times before the devil left.

You need to articulate your case as in a court of law. For you to win a case in court you need to lay out your case line by line, supporting it by the law of the land and similar cases in the past (precedence). Knowing that you are innocent and that you have a right to victory is not enough. You need to justify your victory. You need to present the part of the law that supports your case.

> *Put me in remembrance: let us plead together: declare thou, that thou mayest be justified.* Isaiah 43:26 KJV

> *State your case, that you may be acquitted…* NKJV

> *Ask me of things to come concerning my sons, and concerning the work of my hands command ye me.* Isaiah 45:11 KJV

The scriptures above relate to us in the new covenant; it follows on with the declaration of Jesus in the New Testament.

> *7 If ye abide in me, and my words abide in you, ye shall ask what ye will, and It shall be done unto you.* John 15:7 KJV

The Greek word translated "ask" here means "demand". You shall "Demand whatsoever ye will and it shall be done unto you," Jesus said, not with a cocky attitude or with arrogance but calling on him to fulfil his part of the deal.

> *For as the heavens are higher than the earth, so are my ways higher than your ways, and my thoughts than your thoughts,*
> *10 For as the rain cometh down, and the snow from heaven, and returneth not thither, but watereth the earth, and maketh it bring forth and bud, that it may give seed to the sower, and bread to the eater:*
> *11 So shall my word be that goeth forth out of my mouth: it shall not return unto me void, but it shall*

accomplish that which I please, and it shall prosper in the thing whereto I sent it. Isaiah 55:9-11 KJV

This is the bedrock and foundation of prayer. It is based on the integrity of the word of God. His faithfulness to keep his part.

7. You need to be **consistent** and **persistent** in prayer.
   You have been made righteous, so you have a blood bought right to have your prayers answered and to stand before God without guilt, shame or inferiority. A knowledge of your rightness is a catalyst for answered prayers. The few key words underlined below are vital in your journey to receiving answers to your prayers.

   The prayer of a righteous person is powerful and effective. James 5:16b (NIV)

   The heartfelt and persistent prayer of a righteous man (believer) can accomplish much [when put into action and made effective by God – it is dynamic and can have tremendous power] AMP

   The earnest (heartfelt, continued) prayer of a righteous man makes tremendous power available [dynamic in its working]. AMPC

   Set aside the time and pray diligently during that time. Don't assume the time; set your clock or your stopwatch.

8. You may need to amplify your prayers with fasting.
   Fasting has been downplayed in the modern charismatic setting. It has become the Cinderella of the church, it has been put on the back burner, however even though fasting does not change God it puts your spirit in a place of alertness and a stronger spiritual position to enforce changes.

Fasting is the practice of self-denial. It is abstinence from food to concentrate on spiritual matters.

I don't claim to understand all that happens spiritually but there are some spiritual dynamics that fasting engages that mere words cannot articulate. Some of the challenges we face will never shift unless our prayers are augmented with fasting.

In Daniel chapter 10, the man Daniel was seeking God's face for 21 days and his persistence in prayer and fasting energised his angel to break through with his answer. I often wonder what would have happened if he gave up on the 10th, 17th or 20th day. His answer had been dispatched on the first day, but it was detained by the devil.

> *11 And he said unto me, O Daniel, a man greatly beloved, understand the words that I speak unto thee, and stand upright: for unto thee am I now sent. And when he had spoken this word unto me, I stood trembling.*
> *12 Then said he unto me, Fear not, Daniel: for **from the first day** that thou didst set thine heart to understand, and to chasten thyself before thy God, thy words were heard, **and I am come for thy words.***
> *13 But the prince of the kingdom of Persia withstood me one and twenty days: but, lo, Michael, one of the chief princes, came to help me; and I remained there with the kings of Persia.* Daniel 10:11-13 KJV

In my testimony I engaged the same principle and five days later my partner showed up. I have since heard of many testimonies to the same effect. It's tough on the flesh but effective spiritually.

> *This kind can come forth by nothing, but by prayer and fasting* Mark 9:29 KJV

His disciples already knew how to pray, and they had seen him cast out devils many times but what makes this one different? What makes it so different that Jesus had to label it 'this kind'. It means there are different kinds and this 'particular' kind had to be addressed with prayers amplified with fasting.

Fasting is very effective when you are facing a challenge that seems unmovable.

> *This is the kind of fasting I have chosen: Loosen the chains of wickedness, untie the straps of the yoke, let the oppressed go free, and break every yoke.*
> Isaiah 58:6 (NOG)

In my next book, *Single But NOT Satisfied – 21 days Prayer Guidelines,* I expand more on the intricacies of prayer and the requirements for a fast to accompany the prayers for a spouse.

9. You may need to pray extensively in the Holy Ghost (tongues). The ministry of the Holy Spirit cannot be over-emphasised in the life of a Christian. While waiting, I engaged in praying in the spirit a minimum of one hour in a day and I mean that literally. I understood that he (the Holy Spirit) knows all solutions and answers so I employed him to assist me in my journey (John 14:16).

> *And I will ask the Father, and he will give you another Helper, to be with you forever.* John 14:16). ESV

> *Then I will ask the Father to send you the Holy Spirit who will help you and always be with you.* CEV

We are tempted many times to keep praying long prayers in our understanding but praying in your known language can be quite limited especially when you do not fully understand the forces and powers that you are up against. Praying in the Holy Spirit is unravelling deep secrets and mysteries and it is a direct contact with the Father.

> *For one who speaks in an unknown tongue does not speak to people but to God; for no one understands him or catches his meaning, but by the Spirit he speaks mysteries [secret truths, hidden things].* 1 Corinthians 14:2 AMP

I urge you to connect with your divine helper. Paul wrote to the Ephesian church to make supplication in the spirit.

> *With all prayer and petition pray [with specific requests] at all times [on every occasion and in every season] in the <u>Spirit</u>.* Ephesians 6:18a AMP

The Holy Spirit helps us to pray accurately, he knows where the provision is, and he is an expert at weaving, networking and connecting. Praying in the spirit is speaking the language he (the Holy Spirit) understands and it helps us articulate our request perfectly. He goes beyond our limitations to the very source and root cause of the issue.

> *In the same way the Spirit also helps our weakness; for we do not know how to pray as we should, but the Spirit Himself intercedes for us with groanings too deep for words.* Roman 8:26 (NASB)

> *…agonising longings which never find words, And God who knows the heart's secrets understands, of course, the Spirit's intention as he prays for those who love God.* Roman 8:26 J B Philips

10. You need to cultivate an attitude of Praise.
    Someone said you may pray amiss, but you cannot praise amiss. When everything else fails, move on to praise. Thank him that

you are a candidate for marriage. If you were terminally ill or out of your mind, marriage would not cross your mind.

He has kept you well, with a sound mind. He surely deserves to be praised. You may not have it yet, but YOU WILL HAVE IT.

When the dust settles you still be standing holding your trophy of victory. One of my favourite scriptures is Psalm 100:4 Thanksgiving is the access to heavens resources. use the password now...

> *Enter with the password: "Thank you!" Make yourselves at home, talking praise. Thank him. Worship him.*
> Psalm 100:4 MSG

Praise will ambush your adversary and make you a candidate for victory.

...you are next in line for a testimony, it is your designated moment.

CHAPTER 10

TESTIMONIES

Testimony 1: Married for the first time at 52

Every girl dreams about marriage and what age they plan to be married, have their children and live happily ever after. But for me, God had another plan which I can't really tell you I whole heartedly agreed to.

When I first started to wait on the Lord for the promise of a life partner in my 20s it wasn't that much of a big deal but as time went on, I started to become concerned. I got to my 30s and I was still fine, then into my 40s it kind of bothered me but I continued to serve the Lord fervently with a dogged faith that said, "even if you don't give me a husband I will still serve you with my life."

I was even determined to serve God more. By God's leading, I went to Bible College when I turned 40 and everyone believed and even I believed I was going to meet my husband in Bible school. The Lord kept on encouraging me as He always has all through my journey that He will not short-change me and that He will do exactly what He promised to do. I never once doubted God's promises, I just was so frustrated about the timing.

I graduated Bible school without meeting my husband; instead I met a guy who turned out to be a false brother, I didn't know it at the time, but God delivered me from him as he has always done in this journey of singleness. During my time in Bible College I met a couple who I helped babysit their children and very quickly we became close because their children loved me so much and I loved them like they were mine as well.

I graduated Bible College and after some years, the Lord spoke to me about going to Nigeria; again everyone believed that I would meet my husband in Nigeria, so after much prayer and making sure it was God, I started to make plans to go. This was a big move for me because I had been in America for 9 years so going back to Nigeria meant starting over again, but such has been the Lord's dealing with me, I have had to start over and over again many times in my life.

I got to Nigeria and it was not easy at all to say the least, five years later the Lord started to talk to me about going back to America; at this time I was so drained emotionally and my hope was almost gone, I had to endure the shame and reproach; but I, like Abraham, hoped against hope and trusted God. Yet again, He has and continues to remain faithful to me all through this journey with Him.

I left for America the next year with a strong faith in God that He would do a great thing. Remember the couple I babysat their children in Bible College? We had lost contact with one another when I moved to Nigeria, so when I got back to America I started looking for them on social media because they had moved from the state where I met them to another state. I eventually found their contact information on Facebook and sent them a text. They were so excited to know that I was in America and they told me that they had started a Church and couldn't wait for me to come and see them. I was so excited about the Church and couldn't wait to go and see them.

I eventually travelled to the state where they were, to see them. The children I used to babysit were all grown, and everyone was just too excited to see me. Every Saturday they had a prayer meeting in their home; they didn't have a big congregation, but the meetings were powerful, and the Holy Spirit moved. A lot of events surrounded what I am about to tell you but there was a particular man that stood out to me whenever he came to the house. My friends had spoken so well about him, just as they have with all others. The Lord has surrounded them with so many faithful and giving people. But this man, every time I see him I always feel like the Holy Spirit is saying to pray for him. It became so much that I called my friend, the wife, and said, "Can I please talk to you?" She was a bit concerned and thought something happened, so we went for a drive and I said, "This man that is in your church, is everything fine with him?" and she asked why, then I said because I always feel the urge to pray for him all the time. She was so excited to the point where she almost drove the car off the road. And I was like, what is going on? But it turned out they had sensed that there was something God was going to do concerning me and this brother. It wasn't as if I was attracted to him, or anything like that, except my friends talked about him being a gentleman, easy going, humble and loves the Lord.

He got saved in their Church and has been so faithful in the things of God. We never did get together before I had to return to Nigeria even though I stayed with my Pastor friends for about 2 months. The job I was planning on getting while in America didn't work out, so again I had to return to Nigeria by which time I was 51 years old. Everyone thought I had gone to America for good and now I was coming back again, so I didn't even tell anyone that I was back in Nigeria because I couldn't bear the shame and disappointment.

I have to say that I have never been so discouraged in my life. Before I left for America, I had given up everything including my apartment, because I was so sure that things would work out in America, so here I am going back to nothing. I got to Nigeria and my friends from America kept in touch with me especially regarding the brother I met. He had gotten into a relationship with another lady in Nigeria even before I met him in America, but my friends had told him to wait on the Lord before he proceeded to marry this lady who he only met online.

Anyway, I picked up my life again in Nigeria, just waiting on the Lord, I couldn't really tell you I prayed because I was emotionally and mentally drained to the point of being so depressed. I hid all of this from people around me including my aunt who I had to stay with at the time. In

February of the new year, I decided to go away on a prayer retreat. A day before I ended the prayer, I got a call suddenly from the brother in America I had met through my friends. He never called me or even showed any interest when I was there because like I said he was in another relationship.

At first, I didn't pick up his call because I was just still emotionally distraught, and I just wanted God to give me specifics; besides, my prayer retreat was not for him or a husband. I had left everything behind me and just wanted God to tell me what he wanted me to do at this point. Anyway, shortly after I got a call from my Pastor friend and I picked up. He said he just wanted to check on me and tell me he had given the brother my contact number.

After the prayer retreat I went back home and after a few days this brother started to talk to me on WhatsApp. We would chat off and on and he would ask me when I intended to come back to America and hoped that when I came back I would stay. Eventually, my Pastor friend called me and said, "Sister Funmi, it's time to come back to America now, this brother keeps asking us about you and when you're coming back. God has settled everything so start making arrangements to come," he said.

At this time, travel tickets to America had sky-rocketed and it was becoming almost impossible for me to come up with the funds for the ticket. Meanwhile this brother would not stop asking my friends when I would be coming, so they finally told him I needed to come up with the funds for the ticket to which he said, "not to worry I will send her the money for the ticket." I was like, God, is this you? And the Lord reminded me what I had said in my heart not even audibly that if this was my husband he would send me the money for the ticket. I had said it in my heart because I didn't want it to seem like I was fleecing God.

By God's grace and assurance, I went back to America in April of the same year; at this time I was 52. Michael proposed to me on the third day I arrived after the Saturday prayer meeting! Didn't say yes right away though. The next day after Church he took me out to dinner because I told him I wanted to talk first, and after asking him so many questions I said YES!

On September 17, in the same year that I was 52, I got married to Michael Olukolade Olaniyi to the Glory of God. I couldn't have asked for a better man to spend the rest of my life with, he was everything I asked God for and even more. The Lord turned everything around for me, turned my mourning into dancing and put a new song in my mouth! There are no words to tell you how blessed I am. I still feel as if I am dreaming. The bible is so true in Psalm 126, "When the Lord turned again the captivity of Zion, (Fumilayo) we were like those that dream. Then was our mouth filled with laughter, and our tongue with singing." All I can say is it's been worth the wait!

As you read or listen to this testimony, you're probably praying the prayer that I prayed many times when I read testimonies about people who got married at my age. God please I don't want to be this age before I get married! To that I say, whenever God does it will be so perfect you will not remember that you are a certain age! The conclusion of it all is to serve God, be faithful to Him and He will astound and embarrass you with blessings you cannot even dream or imagine! All the Glory be to God forever and ever!

Funmi Olaniyo
Virginia USA

Testimony 2: Divorced but remembered

All was well, I was young and had just gotten married to a wonderful young Christian man. Early married life was great and we both served the Lord in our newly found Church in Amsterdam.

A few years later, marriage had its usual swing of little ups and downs. Short-term unemployment and then the joys of finding work, medical challenges and then the glory of getting healed, family feuds and then fun-filled reunions, occasional disagreements followed by blissful vacations...

We had great friends, bought our own home, volunteered at the local library while flourishing in our jobs. We were best friends, learning and growing together in love, in Christ and in intimacy.

We thought about having kids, but we figured we were still young, there was lots of time, we can wait…

And then he slowly started to withdraw. He became more reflective, staying late at work, watching late-night TV, less interested in social activities, feeling unaccomplished and general dissatisfaction with the path of his life.

It was a phase l thought, until one day he decided it was over. He needs to fulfil his dreams, he desires renewed happiness, he needs a new chapter… soon enough he turned to God for strength, briefly apologized, packed up his stuff and left me. And I never saw him again…

I was devastated! The shock and trauma of separation almost derailed my faith in God. Did I not pray enough? Did I not fast enough? Did I not give enough? Or was I just not good enough? Did I ignore any red flags during our dating? Should I have gotten pregnant earlier in the marriage instead of waiting? Did I…?? Should l…?? Can…l??

I spent the next few years refusing to give up, alone fighting and praying and confessing and crying… God hates divorce, He will surely soften the heart of stone, intervene and oh what a joyful and glorious reconciliation that will be.

I found strength in hope, I even started to plan the reconciliation party and lest l forget I longed for the restoration of intimacy. To digress further, being celibate before marriage was relatively easy for me, what you don't know much of you don't miss was my motto. My body was the temple of the Holy Ghost and so it was to remain. I was not concerned about that area when he left, I was confident that returning to celibacy should be easy… eeerh not quite the same after marriage, because you've developed in another area and cannot simply erase that!

However, I was determined before God to remain celibate again, I can do all things through Christ who strengthens me and so He did, Glory to God!

I drifted from denial to determination to defeat and then depression. I was hanging on to the word of truth and to the wedding band on my finger seeking prayer partners and signing up for Christian marriage fighters; 'Rejoice Marriage Ministries' was one of the good ones to be exact!

After four difficult years of despair and desperation and finally realizing there were no further options left to persuade him towards reconciliation, l was forced to sign the divorce papers which I received at work and forwarded immediately to my lawyer before I changed my mind again.

My mind was numb afterwards. It was a Friday, a festive weekend and my close friend was waiting to pick me up for an evening of detox at her place… a couple of other girlfriends came to join us later that night.

We talked, we laughed, we prayed and we sang praises. Then we reminisced about the wonders of marriage and deliberated on the contrast in characteristics between women and men. We finally cried at the reality of the end of an era…..the end of my marriage, a broken covenant relationship!

As girls usually do we re-grouped, gave thanks and they all encouraged me with words of life & hope. We then spent the rest of the time in good spirits, listening to good music and feasting on comfort food until the wee hours of the morning.

I entered the 'Singles' world with a constant sense of shame. I felt I had my one chance in marriage, but I blew it. If he left, it must have been my fault. Nothing anyone said could convince me otherwise. I was scared of remaining single, it wasn't what I wanted. However, I was scared of getting married again, I truly believed God would be displeasing of that. I was confused!!

How can I trust myself to hear again from God to pick the right person for me?

Do we really hear from God for a partner?? Or should we be picking for ourselves??

If a Christian can fall apart, what are the guarantees for a successful marriage?? Maybe I should pick a non-Christian this time and try to convert him, it'll be very easy for him to get saved, especially seeing my devotion to the Lord, it will win him over and I can kill two birds with one stone!!

I wondered in fear and eventually a year later I went on my first date. He said he was a Christian, but I sensed deep down he really wasn't. He'd drive 100km to pick me up every Sunday morning go to church, he shouted the loudest Amen during the preaching, he cried during worship, gave money faithfully and once reprimanded me for chewing gum in church, wow, what devotion!!

He sat at the back cheering me on as I led the youth choir rehearsals on Tuesdays… and of course he was the doting gentleman, impressing me with dinners and romantic gifts!! This must for sure be the one!!

Then the demand for intimacy began, I wasn't too shocked to be honest, but I thought I could hold him off and keep the godly interest going. He was persuasive and determined. The more I resisted the more he persisted. We argued constantly over the scriptures, he truly believed intimacy was a gift of God and healthy for the body to function and that God understood...

But as the days passed on to weeks, I realized my fighting was futile as I blatantly refused to compromise, I prayed relentlessly asking God to change his heart. However, salvation is personal, it has to come from the individual, so l had no other choice but to end the relationship, lift up my head and put my trust in the Lord!

Our journey in Christ is not just about our victories but about overcoming our challenges. The desire to be married is a gift from God but the pursuit of this desire is where the challenge is...

'Be ye not unequally yoked' is the first commandment of dating, so I decided to spend my time with single Christians starting from my Church singles group.

I attended social events, volunteered at functions and even took a 10-week marriage preparedness class. No real interest from the guys initially until I finally met Jeff, a good Christian man who seemed to tick all the boxes.

After a few weeks though, I wanted to hear from God about where the friendship was going but nothing came. Jeff was very committed, but I still wasn't sure. He loved the Lord and was a true gentleman, but I had no peace about him. I always wondered how he would fit into my family? Not very well, I could see that red flag bright and shiny, I backed off and moved on.

Then came Gerard who I met at a Christian outing, we clicked quickly, he was a good Christian, we attended fellowship and social events together and he was definitely looking into the future for us until that faithful day he picked me up and had cigarette breath on him, needless to say that was it for me...

I didn't date again until four years later when I met the one...

How do you know if a guy is the right one? How do you meet good Christian men? Do you need a checklist? Is there the perfect one for you or do you reach out to the best one and make him perfect?

These were the thoughts in my head as I dabbled into different social gatherings hoping to meet the right one…

Singles club, Singles Christmas dance, Singles cafe, Online Christian dating, Christian speed dating, Light club (Christian night club), Christian concerts, Singles picnic, Singles horseback riding, Singles meet-up and on and on…

I guarded my heart with numerous scriptures and watched the red flags with scrutiny as I met different types of guys in the next few years, but I never dated anyone.

Cast your bread upon the waters the Bible says, sow in the morning, afternoon and evening. Faith without works is dead… I searched everywhere but nothing came up!

Hope deferred makes the heart sick, I got weary and tired and discouraged so I stopped the search and just cried to the Lord every night…

I focused on ministry and stopped looking. I was done. If the Lord can hear my cry, then it will happen. I held on tightly to Luke 18 and cried all the more, night after night, determined to weary Him as the widow wearied the Judge…

And then on that faithful day, a married Christian friend came to visit me and said she knew of a single guy living thousands of miles away from me who might be a match. My red flag and scary bells started to ring loudly as I was not an advocate for long-distance relationships. She gave me his profile which, though admirable, didn't really tweak my interest as I was already biased.

However, I was wise enough to pray and to ask God to help me to be open-minded. This time I wanted to see things as God did. I believed in

God, His ways are not our ways, but He brings us to our expected end. I already had my list before God, which was categorized into: "must have", "deal breaker", "nice to have" and "a little icing on the cake". So I trusted my friend's judgement and asked her to give him my number...

The first few weeks of phone calls and texts were quite good. He was funny, witty, engaging, pleasant, a true gentleman and definitely in no rush to define the friendship which was a pleasant surprise.

Although we had a 6-hour time zone difference, he always made time to connect every single day. We prayed together online, we laughed at each other, listened to Christian contemporary music, shared old-school classics and had bible devotions to strengthen our faith.

By the third month of long-distance dating we were experts at playing online Scrabble all day long. Many times, I'd pause at work to play my turn and I'd hear the click of his turn playing late in the middle of the night.

We cooked together via Skype, watched the World Cup together via FaceTime, chatted on SMS endlessly all day and stared amusingly at each other through our phones wondering however did this relationship happen...

On the fourth month he flew over to visit me, we finally met for the very first time at the airport and simply clicked instantly. It was like the Lord was preparing our hearts in our separate countries and then He match-made us the instant we met. We were open, our faith was strong, our trust in the Lord was secure and our hearts melted! I knew instantly he was the one.

The Lord heard my cries and he answered exceeding, abundantly and above, icing on the cake inclusive!!

The next year was filled with love and joy and praises and gratitude to the Lord who alone is the way maker. He ordered our steps through our treasured friend and He brought us together to bless our lives.

We flew back and forth on visits, met each other's family, enriching our bond enormously. And then on Valentine's Day the following year he flew into town and proposed to me, no more back and forth, it was time to be together as one! Right there and then, we picked the traditional engagement date, the wedding date and decided on our honeymoon cruise… we were married 8 months later.

When it comes to meeting the right partner, the wisdom of man is foolishness unto the Lord. There is no right method for finding the right partner. The only method that is sure is to pray for the Lord to open your heart and order your steps.

It is good to trust in the Lord and to lean not to our own understanding. It is good to wait patiently for the Lord and not compromise on His ways just for a few minutes of satisfaction. And after 14 years of celibacy, I can honestly say, it was well worth the wait!!

To God be the glory for the things He has done!

Tracy Coker
Maryland, USA

Testimony 3: Single but NOT satisfied

I was born into a middle-class family in west Africa and had all that I needed and was well schooled. I got born again at 15 years old and was on fire for God. I continued with this until my university days. I graduated from university and proceeded to writing my professional accounting exams. My friends had started getting married at this stage and I was attending weddings but was never the bride. I did not date and was not really bothered as such. I attended a good church and was active in church. My friends and I pioneered an outreach at the commercial hub of the state, we won many to the Lord and established them in the faith.

In my $25^{th}/26^{th}$ year, there were multiple tragedies in the family and I relocated to London, England. At this point in time I started dating a guy, but we drifted apart, and we went our separate ways. I migrated to Canada when I was 29 years old in search of a better life and greener pastures.

I again helped pioneer the church in Toronto and was active in intersession and outreaches. The church was a great church and taught me about the Holy Spirit and his personality; I am eternally grateful for this foundation, however the church did not place an emphasis on marriage, so it was not unusual to find many single ladies in the church leadership both locally and globally. The Holy Spirit said to me that his ministry is to endorse anything that is preached in a church. If you preach healings you will see healings, if you preach finances, people will get financial breakthrough. God always confirms his word with signs following.

I met a chap in Toronto, I thought he was 'the one' but it was only afterwards that I found out he was a pro at leading people on. In my 33rd to 35th year, I struggled with why I was not married; I prayed and fasted often, even though I seemed to have everything working for me in every area, there did not seem to be any breaks in the marriage area. I have detailed some more of my story in the introduction.

In my 36th year I was divinely led by the Holy Spirit to relocate back to London, this did not seem logical as I had all that I could desire in Canada, I had a six-figure income, a good Condo, drove a nice car and had good friends both in and out of the church, but after confirmations from the Lord and many different people that I respect, I moved to the UK on the 10th of October of my 36th year.

I joined a good church as soon as possible in London but kept my ear out to hearing God. I got an excellent job, bought my house, drove a nice car but still no man.

When 40 was approaching, I realised I knew I had to take some drastic steps. I enrolled in a Bible school and equipped myself spiritually and strategically for this hindrance that I realised was not from God. I did some days of prayer and fasting and had intermittent breakthroughs. I dated four guys in a space of 24 months but none of them lasted or translated into anything permanent.

When I turned 42, I understood that this would take radical steps to remediate my singleness. I was sick and tired of being single. I began to seek God afresh, to get clear instructions on the way forward. I knew I had to do what I had not done before. I had fasted in the past, many times over but this was different, I embarked on a 21-day fast with serious praying in the spirit. Sometimes I prayed in the spirit for 2 hours at a stretch during this time. I rounded up my prayers and fasting the first week in December. My husband showed up five days afterwards and we were married 10 months afterwards.

God still answers prayers…

Funmi QJ
London, England

Lightning Source UK Ltd.
Milton Keynes UK
UKHW041348211118
332683UK00001B/155/P